Published by Creative Education
123 South Broad Street, Mankato, Minnesota 56001
Creative Education is an imprint of The Creative Company

Designed by Stephanie Blumenthal
Production Design by The Design Lab

Photos by: Allsport USA, AP/Wide World Photos, NU Sports Information,
SportsChrome, Sports Photo Masters, Jeff Tuttle, UPI/Corbis-Bettmann

Library of Congress Cataloging-in-Publication Data

Griffin, Gwen, 1957–
Barry Sanders / by Gwen Griffin
p. cm. – (Ovations)
Summary: Examines the personal life and football career of the
well-known running back for the Detroit Lions and the NFL's 1989
Rookie of the Year.
ISBN 0-88682-938-0

1. Sanders, Barry, 1968– –Juvenile literature. 2. Football
players–United States–Biography–Juvenile literature. 3.
Detroit Lions (Football team)–Juvenile literature. [1. Sanders,
Barry, 1968-. 2. Football players. 3. Afro-Americans–Biography.]
I. Title. II. Series: Ovations (Mankato, Minn.)

GV939.S18G75   1999
796.332'092–dc21
[B]   98-47751

First Edition

2   4   6   8   9   7   5   3   1

OVATIONS

BARRY

SANDERS

BY GWEN GRIFFIN

Creative Education

REFLECTIONS

On a crisp, sunny afternoon in late fall, sounds of football helmets and pads hitting together fill the air. A whistle blows. A coach yells for a time-out. There's a player down on the field. As his teammates crowd around him, the injured player groans. "He wasn't supposed to push me down from behind," the fourth-grader cries. The coach wipes away tears and dirt and sends his players back into the game. "Do your best!" he says. "That's what counts!" And another future legend runs back to the line of scrimmage to make another play on Barry Sanders Field.

An hour later, in the Silverdome in Pontiac, Michigan, the Detroit Lions are engaged in a fierce battle with the Chicago Bears. With the game tied and time running out, the Lions'

quarterback takes the snap and hands the ball to Barry Sanders. The Pro-Bowl back cuts hard to the right, his eyes wide in search of a hole in the wall of Chicago jerseys. One seems to open, and he darts into it with blinding quickness.

Suddenly, two linebackers and a safety converge on Barry, and it looks like he will go down under their combined weight. Barry's powerful legs, however, withstand the assault, and with an incredible off-balance spin, he breaks free from the gang tackle. As Barry sprints the last 30 yards into the end zone, television broadcasters shout in disbelief, the Bears' coach slams his clipboard to the turf, and Lions fans rain their thundering praise down on Barry.

Number 20, for his part, simply hands the ball to the official a second before being mobbed by his teammates. He doesn't spike the ball or dance; he never has. Barry does all of his dancing where it counts—around defenders on the way to the end zone and all over the National Football League record books.

Great vision, cat-like quickness, and break-away speed have made Barry the NFL's most dangerous and exciting running back for a decade.

EVOLUTION

When Barry Sanders was a young boy, he dreamed of being a starting guard on the United States Olympic basketball team.

Born on July 16, 1968, in Wichita, Kansas, Barry grew up in a family with eight sisters and two brothers. His father William worked as a roofer and remodeler and was a die-hard Cleveland Browns fan.

When his brother Byron was playing PeeWee football, Barry wanted to play, too. But his father forbade him from joining. When Barry joined anyway, his father said, "If you want it that bad, go ahead and play."

As a fourth-grader, Barry played football with the Greater Wichita Youth Football League and was an outstanding athlete even at nine years old. The first time he carried the ball in his first game for the Beech Street

Barons, he scored on a 70-yard sweep. Barry's father was watching Byron's game on another field when a friend brought him the news. "What are you talking about?" William said. "Barry can't even play football." But Barry made an impression on everyone who saw him play that day.

Although he didn't play any organized sports while attending Hadley Junior High, Barry still followed football. When he wasn't devoting time to his studies, he enjoyed watching some very talented— and small—running backs, including Terry Metcalf of the St. Louis Cardinals, Tony Dorsett of the Dallas Cowboys, and Billy Sims of the Detroit Lions. But Barry still liked basketball better.

By the time Barry entered North High School in the fall of 1983, he knew his dreams of basketball were over. "The only problem is I stopped growing after awhile. I'm not 6-foot-6-inches—I'm 5-foot-8-inches. I can jump like Michael Jordan, but I'm not as tall as him, so there went my dream."

But another dream took its place. Barry and his brother Byron dreamed of playing for the Los Angeles Raiders, and one of their football heroes was Marcus Allen. "We watched the Raiders religiously. When they lost games, it would almost bring us to tears," Barry said.

Although Barry dreamed of basketball stardom as a young-ster, he soon realized that his stocky frame and quick feet were best suited for the football field.

During his first two seasons of football in high school, Barry was a defensive back. He seldom played those first two years and never even carried the ball once. At 5-foot-5 and 140 pounds, Barry was often overlooked because of his small size. During his junior year, he had a chance to play at tailback, the same position his older brother Byron, who was a senior, played. Barry chose not to compete with his brother for the position. Byron graduated and went to college at Northwestern University, and North High School hired a new football coach.

When tryouts came around for his senior year, Barry told the new head coach, Dale Burkholder, that he wanted to be a wide receiver. The coach just nodded and looked at a player he thought was too short. When he saw Barry run the 40-yard dash in 4.4 seconds, he changed his mind.

In his third game of the 1985 season, Barry scored the first time he was handed the ball. He ran for 274 yards and four touchdowns in the fourth game. Although he started only five games as a senior, he still rushed for more than 1,000 yards.

Barry's mother Shirley missed many of his Friday night football games when he was growing up. Friday night was reserved for choir practice at Paradise Baptist Church, and religion was an important part of the Sanders' household. The close-knit family went to church every Sunday. Even though she didn't get to see her son play very much, Barry's mom is still a very important person in his life. "She was hard-working," Barry said, "and a great inspiration for me to work hard." A soft-spoken woman, Shirley has always been very close to Barry. "Barry, he used to make me mad because he was just like his mother," William remembered. "Looks like her. Quiet like her."

It was also during Barry's senior year that he showed what kind of a person he was when it came to sharing the glory of the team. In his last regular-season game, Wichita North was pummeling crosstown rival Wichita East 48–0 at the end of three quarters. Realizing that Barry could win the City League rushing title if he stayed in the game, Coach Burkholder let his star know about the situation. Instead of returning to the field,

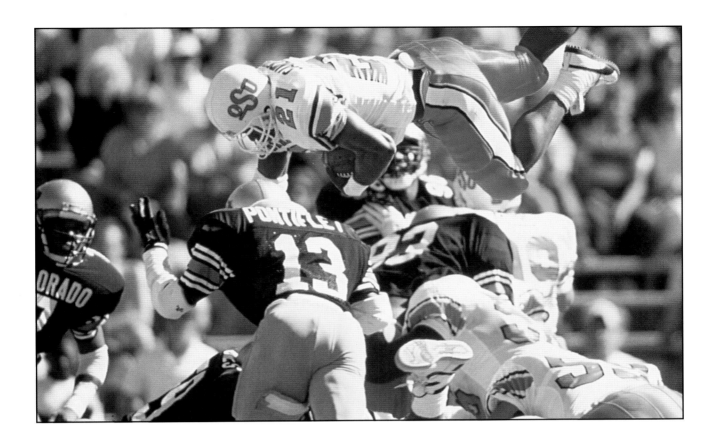

Barry responded, "I'm not worried about that rushing title thing. Let the other kids play." But the titles would come his way after all. Barry was named to the All-City and All-State teams for his efforts.

Many recruiters considered Barry too short to play football at the college level. Even though he rushed for 1,561 yards (other sources say 1,417), averaged 9.3 yards per carry, and scored 21 touchdowns in his senior season, most colleges were not impressed. One recruiter told Barry's coach, "We don't need another midget."

In the end, only Oklahoma State University and Wichita State University offered Barry a football scholarship. Besides Oklahoma State, the only NCAA Division I-A schools that expressed real interest were Iowa State and Tulsa University. Barry chose Oklahoma State University because it had the best business program of the schools he was interested in, and he planned on majoring in business. OSU planned on using Barry mainly as a kickoff and punt returner and awarded him a scholarship in 1986.

Barry played three seasons with the Oklahoma State Cowboys. As a sophomore, he led the nation in kickoff returns and was named the 1987

After a relatively quiet high school football career, Barry exploded into the national spotlight at Oklahoma State, soaring over the competition as a kick returner in his first two seasons.

Sporting News All-American Kick Returner. He also won the NCAA Kickoff Returning Title with a 31.3 yards-per-return average. Playing behind another future NFL great, Thurman Thomas, Barry didn't play a full season until his junior year, when he was moved from return man to running back. His record-breaking career was underway.

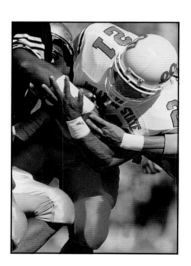

Barry returned the opening kickoff of two consecutive season-opening games for touchdowns, becoming the only player in NCAA history to accomplish that feat. He set or tied 34 NCAA records and set numerous OSU records, including the most 100-yard games in a single season (12) and the longest kickoff return (100 yards, which he did three times). In a sport where few players achieve 300-yard games, Barry had four such performances in his junior season. The leading rusher in Oklahoma State history with 3,575 yards, Barry was also the school's top scorer with 56 career touchdowns.

When asked about Barry's talent, OSU head coach Pat Jones said, "Sanders isn't the fastest college back in the country, and he's not the biggest. But he combines strength, willpower, and an uncanny ability to wriggle, shift, and explode into high gear from a dead stop." In his third and final season at Oklahoma State, Barry led the nation with 2,628 yards, which is still an NCAA single-season record. He also exploded into the national spotlight as the 1988 Heisman Trophy winner.

In post-season play, the Cowboys went to the Hula Bowl and Barry had another chance to shine. He ran for 222 yards and five touchdowns. Just three yards short of breaking the bowl rushing record, Barry was given the chance to return to the game. Not worried about breaking records, he chose to remain on the sidelines and cheer on his Cowboys teammates.

The cheers would continue for Barry in 1988. He was honored as the College Football Player-of-the-Year, voted to the All-American team, and named the Maxwell Club College Football Player of the Year. It seemed like it couldn't get any better for Barry.

Much of the sports world was surprised when Barry did not return to Oklahoma State for his senior year. He renounced his eligibility in order to

Barry played like a giant as a college senior in 1988, leading the Cowboys to the Hula Bowl and earning All-American honors and the coveted Maxwell Award.

play professionally. He decided that, by playing professionally, he could help his family overcome the financial hardships they had faced through the years.

It was during a pre-draft workout in Stillwater, Oklahoma, in 1989 that Detroit Lions head coach Wayne Fontes saw Barry. Dallas and Green Bay had the first two picks in the upcoming NFL draft and had almost settled on Troy Aikman and Tony Mandarich as their choices. Even after winning the Heisman Trophy, Barry still had not made much of an impression on the NFL coaches and scouts, including those of the Detroit Lions, who had the draft's third pick. During that workout, though, Barry surprised the coaches and scouts with some amazing statistics: a 4.36-second 40-yard dash, a 42-inch vertical jump, and an 11-foot standing broad jump. He also bench-pressed 225 pounds 21 times. After Barry's performance, Coach Fontes said to the other coaches and scouts, "My running back won't be doing anything else today. He's going to Detroit. Thank you for coming."

In his first season as a Detroit Lion, Barry eclipsed the club's single-season rushing mark with 1,470 yards, a record that also broke the rookie mark previously held by football legend Billy Sims. Barry wears jersey number 20 for the Lions, the same

After Detroit coach Wayne Fontes, middle, brought Barry to the Lions with the third pick in the 1989 NFL draft, the young star broke the team's rookie rushing record set by former great Billy Sims, opposite top.

number worn by Sims. When Barry was younger, Sims had been one of his favorite players. With 14 rushing touchdowns, Barry was voted consensus 1989 Rookie of the Year and went to the Pro Bowl. That year, he also gave each of the Lions' offensive linemen a Rolex watch, valued at more than $10,000. Each one was inscribed on the back: "Thanks for a great 1989 season—Barry Sanders."

Difficult to tackle because of his compact size and great speed, Barry's first year in the NFL was sensational. And his opponents had a hard time believing his skill on the field. At one point in a game between the Lions and the Minnesota Vikings that year, Vikings head coach Jerry Burns called a time-out and asked officials to check Barry's arms and uniform for silicon or some other slippery substance. Barry seemed to be "slipping off" of would-be tacklers in the Vikings defense. The officials carefully inspected Barry and his uniform and found nothing.

But the Vikings weren't the only players Barry embarrassed. San Francisco 49ers All-Pro quarterback Steve Young said, "Barry will flat out embarrass you. He can change direction and do things no one else has ever been able to do. It should be illegal."

In the final game of his rookie year against the Atlanta Falcons, Barry was only 10 yards behind the Kansas City Chiefs' Christian Okoye for the NFL rushing title. Head coach Wayne Fontes asked Barry if he wanted to return to the game to break the record. Barry declined, wanting to give veteran backup Tony Paige more playing time. The Lions were leading 31–24 over the Falcons, and he had already scored three touchdowns and rushed for 158 yards. He didn't see the need to keep carrying the ball. "When everyone is out for statistics—you know, individual fulfillment—that's when trouble starts," Barry said. "I don't want to ever fall victim to that."

But if you ask his mother, Shirley Sanders would say that her son's greatest accomplishment that year was the gift he gave to Paradise Baptist Church. Barry donated 10 percent of his $2.1 million signing bonus to his hometown church.

Barry continued to set records for the Lions, claiming the NFL rushing title in 1990 with 1,304 yards on 255 carries. In 1991, he was the NFL touchdown leader with 17 end-zone appearances. And by 1992, he had played in four consecutive Pro Bowl games.

Barry's ability to cut in any direction at full speed makes him the most elusive runner in the history of professional football.

With so much going for him, Barry seemed to be on top of the world. But few people knew what was happening behind the scenes.

Barry's sister Nancy came to live with him in Michigan in 1991. Perhaps the most talented member of the family, Nancy was the star in the Sanders household with a beautiful singing voice and a talent for the piano. "She sang everything," Barry remembered. "We'd sit and talk and someone would say something that would remind my sisters of a song, and then on cue, they'd all start singing." Much like her father, Nancy was also direct, outspoken, and funny. Whenever one of the kids was up to something, it was Nancy's job to break the news to their dad.

Unfortunately, Nancy had developed scleroderma, a disease that causes swelling and thickening of the skin. No one knew she was dying when she moved to Michigan. She helped Barry with his home. "She organized everything," Barry said. "The disease made it hard for her to open doors. But she was so independent. Even though she couldn't do a lot of stuff, she was determined to do it." Nancy died November 6, 1991, when she was 27 years old.

Dubbed the "Lion King," Barry led Detroit to the NFC championship game in 1992. Washington, however, buried the Lions in that contest 42–10 and went on to win the Super Bowl. In 1993, Barry was named the Lions Quarterback Club Offensive MVP. He was leading the NFL with 1,052 yards before he sprained his left knee and missed the last five games of the season.

Although he has carried the ball at least 243 times and as many as 342 times a season, Barry has avoided serious injuries for most of his career. Out on the field, Barry's goal is simple: "Survival. The idea is to avoid being hit," Barry declared. "It's a serious game, and I'm serious about the way I play." Lions coach Bobby Ross sees it this way: "Barry takes good care of himself, he's in good shape, and he's a conscientious person when it comes to preparing."

But, even as conscientious as he is, Barry found himself in a difficult situation in 1994. Early in his career, Barry had spoken about his religious beliefs against premarital sex and had made a video in 1991 for Athletes for Abstinence. Then, three years later, he fathered a son, Barry James III, without being married. "Now I realize more than any other time in my life how important it is not to have a kid out of wedlock," Barry commented. Barry James lives

with his mother, Aletha House, in Oklahoma City. "I'll be seeing him a lot during the off-season," Barry said. "I know he mentions me a lot and he really likes daddy. That's cool. I like that."

Barry has gone through a lot in the past few years, and although he is a very public figure, he tries to keep as much of his life private as he can. "You do what's right," Barry said. That includes being a responsible father, building a new home for his parents in Wichita, and paying college tuition for his brothers and sisters. While he has many opportunities for endorsements, he's careful about what he chooses. He even made sure that his contract with Nike included a clause that requires the company to send his former high school football coach 60 pairs of shoes each year for the team. Barry also helps the Oakland County, Michigan, Special Olympics with his "P.A.Y.-by-Play" program, in which sponsors donate a penny for each yard he gains. Teammate Kevin Glover said, "His actions speak louder than any words ever could. I think everybody's different. You have to be your own person, and he's been great doing that since day one."

In 10 seasons in the NFL, Barry has rushed for 1,000 yards and gone to the Pro Bowl every year. Although he has reached the point in his career when most players begin to slow down, Barry is still going strong. In 1997, he gained 2,053 yards on 335 attempts and set yet another NFL record by racking up 14 straight 100-yard games. By the end of the 1998 season, he needed just 1,458 yards to pass Walter Payton as the league's all-time leading rusher. At his current pace of 1,527 yards per season, barring any injuries or mishaps, it is almost certain that Barry will set the new NFL record.

But breaking records is not Barry's biggest concern. "I just feel that I'll play as long as it's fun and it's what I prefer to do with my life," he said. In spite of being told he was too small, Barry has been setting records on the football field since he was a fourth-grader in Wichita, Kansas. He will go down as one of the most legendary running backs in NFL history, but Barry is most focused on making the game fun for himself and football fans everywhere.

Once thought of as too small for football, Barry has catapulted to the top of the list of today's football heroes—both on and off the field.

V O I C E S

O N   H I S   M O T I V A T I O N :

"Considering my size, I knew I had
to be creative on the field. I've taken
that philosophy everywhere I go. Learn
your limitations and learn to work
around them. Recognize your strengths
and capitalize on them."

Barry Sanders

"I don't play for the records. I play
to win."

Barry Sanders

"You play because you enjoy it and
that's the single most important factor.
After that, if you enjoy it, it stands to
reason that your goal would be to be
the best at it."

Barry Sanders

"I never knew how good I could be because everyone was always telling me I was too small to be much."

Barry Sanders

On His Ability:

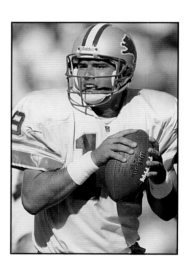

"Barry's an amazing player. He's done things in games I've never seen anybody do. He's stopped dead in his tracks at times and makes some miraculous move and scores a 60-yard TD. It's fun to watch him, and you have to be careful not to get caught watching him too much. He makes, on a routine basis, big plays. You never know what's gonna happen when he has the ball."

Scott Mitchell, NFL quarterback

"As a pure runner, he's the best in the business—great balance, quickness, and vision."

> Pat Summerall,
> football commentator

"It's remarkable. I mean it's almost breathtaking to see him do the things that he does against the best athletes in the world."

> Marcus Allen,
> Former NFL running back

"He's blessed with abilities that not many people are blessed with. He's the best in the league. I want to meet the guy that can stop him."

> Jason Belser,
> NFL safety

"Sanders defies the laws of physics and gravity. I've never been awed by a back before, but that guy is just great."

> Darryl Talley,
> Former NFL linebacker

"When you talk to defensive players . . . the guy they still fear the most is Barry Sanders."

> John Madden,
> football commentator
> and former NFL coach

With the support of his former and current teammates, Barry has earned the admiration of today's defensive players and such former football greats as Marcus Allen, top.

"He's a good young man. Inside his own self he wants to do what's right. We taught all of our children to make a commitment and never bring shame to your family. Barry's done well. I'd like to think we did something right."

Shirley Sanders, Barry's mother

"My father doesn't realize that although we appear to be reserved, no one in the world can intimidate any of his children because of the way he was. He loved us, and that's the difference."

Byron Sanders, Barry's brother

"There was never any pressure [to play sports]. My pressure was to make up my bed, don't hit my sisters, and 'C'mon boy, let's go work on this roof.'"

Barry Sanders

"You do what's right."

Barry Sanders

"It's not how important life is, but how important the experience of living life, with close ones and relatives, and how important that time is."

Barry Sanders

Like his older brother Byron, left, Barry has always run with a confidence and unselfishness gained from his tight family upbringing.

"Christianity affects your whole life. I feel I'm more competitive, a better player, but off the field is where there is always a battle. That's where the power came. I was always successful on the field, but now I'm successful off the field too."

Barry Sanders

ON HIS RECORD-BREAKING CAREER:

"Any time he touches the ball, it's a highlight reel. The player most fun to watch, and by far the most dangerous player in the game today, is Barry Sanders. He is just remarkable."

Marcus Allen,
Former NFL running back

"I've never thought about records. I'm just out there running."

Barry Sanders

"Barry Sanders is the best in the game and the best that I have ever seen. I'm always putting Barry in a class by himself. It's Barry and then it's everybody else. Barry's in a class of his own."

Terrell Davis,
NFL running back

As a 10-time Pro-Bowler at the top of his game, Barry has set the highest of standards for such up-and-coming stars as running back Terrell Davis, bottom.

"He is going to be what everybody else is compared to."

Walter Payton,
Former NFL running back

ON BEING COMPARED TO JIM BROWN:

"Let me tell you this here. O. J. Simpson, Tony Dorsett, Franco Harris, Eric Dickerson, the kid from Dallas—Emmitt Smith—they're only imitations of Jim Brown. Even Barry."

William Sanders

"My father is my biggest fan and biggest supporter. But like a lot of kids, he grew up in Wichita, Kansas, listening to the radio and listening to Jim Brown and the Cleveland Browns. Nothing in his mind will be able to eclipse those memories he has as a kid. I know as far as he is concerned, I'll always be second to Jim Brown. But I can live with that."

Barry Sanders

"Barry Sanders is unbelievable. I have the greatest respect for him. His ability is unparalleled, and he transcends time."

Jim Brown,
Former NFL running back

With a humility rarely seen in professional sports, Barry has put together a career that will place him among—if not ahead of—such all-time greats as Walter Payton, left, and Jim Brown, bottom.

OVATIONS